Dedications

To Brookie and Charlotte, my own Ukulele Girls, and Liam and Scott-
You are all the perfect band mates! Love you. And to Tracy, for being
the inspiring accompaniment I needed.

- J.B.

To all the keiki everywhere, use your talents with pride, be brave in
your creativity and never be afraid to shine !

- K.P.

Published and distributed by

ISLAND HERITAGE®
175 Kahelu Avenue, Unit #4
Mililani, Hawai'i 96789
Orders: (800) 468-2800
Information: (808) 564-8800
Fax: (808) 564-8877
welcometotheislands.com

ISBN: 1-61710-503-1, EAN: 978-1-61710-503-6
First Edition, First Printing—2022
AFO 221401

ALORA and her ʻUkulele ♪

Written by Jill Boldt
Illustrated by Kristi Petosa-Sigel

ISLAND HERITAGE®

Aloha! I'm Alora and I love to play music. I take my ʻukulele everywhere I go - the beach, the store, on walks, in the car, and even to Tūtū's house.

Tonight we're having a neighborhood lū'au and I've been asked to play my 'ukulele for everyone! I'm nervous to play by myself, so I've decided to start a band. I'm going for a walk to see who I can find, but first - breakfast!

“Momma, one cinnamon sugar to go, please.”

“One malasada just for you, Alora,” says Momma as she hands me a warm sugar doughnut. “Please stop at Tūtū’s house and invite her to the lū‘au. Be careful on your walk. I hope you can find someone to play with you at the lū‘au.”

“Mahalo,” I say and give her a sugary kiss as I grab my ‘ukulele and head out the door.

I walk out the back porch to the trail that leads to Tūtū's house. The ocean is calm today and I see the Hawaiian spinner dolphins playing in the distance. Will they want to join my band? I walk out onto the dock and start to play my ʻukulele.

"Aloha, spinner dolphins! Would you like to join my band?" I ask as three of them swim up to me. They poke their heads out of the water and say, "Click-click squeak-squeak," and then begin spinning and twirling to my strumming. They are beautiful dancers, but not bandmates.

"Mahalo," I sing out as I head back to the trail. "A hui hou!"

I walk along the shore, strumming and humming, when I notice a Hawaiian monk seal following alongside me in the water.

“Aloha, monk seal! Would you like to join my band?” The monk seal pops out his head, opens his mouth wide and says, “Aaah, gaah, snort, BURP,” and then rolls onto his belly. He has a nice deep voice, but he is not a bandmate.

“Mahalo,” I sing out as I head back to the trail. “A hui hou!”

Next, I notice wide tracks that lead from the water to some trees. I follow them and come upon a Hawaiian green sea turtle.

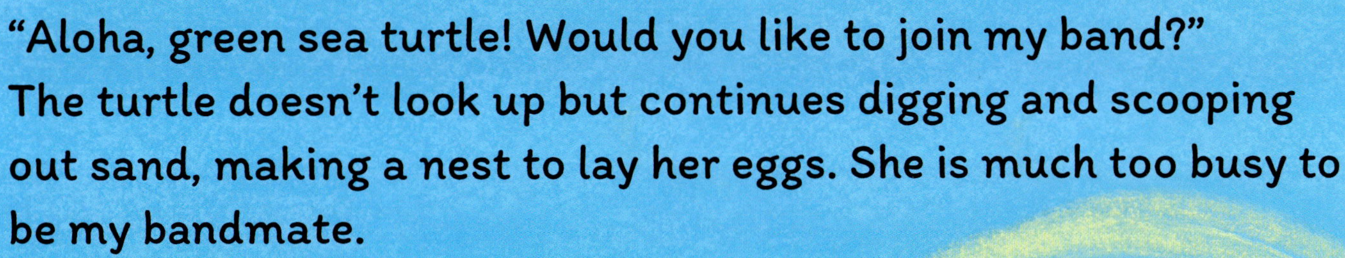

"Aloha, green sea turtle! Would you like to join my band?" The turtle doesn't look up but continues digging and scooping out sand, making a nest to lay her eggs. She is much too busy to be my bandmate.

"Mahalo," I sing out as I head back to the trail. "A hui hou!"

I find a tall tree to rest under and begin to play a song. I hear something above me and look closely as I spot a teeny, tiny Hawaiian hoary bat. I had woken him up and he is letting me know.

“Aloha, hoary bat! Would you like to join my band?” The bat doesn’t move from his roosting branch but replies, “Hiss, hiss, hiss.” He needs his sleep and is too tired to be my bandmate.

“Mahalo,” I sing out as I head back to the trail. “A hui hou!”

I am almost to Tūtū's house when two Hawaiian nēnē geese wobble over to me. "Aloha, nēnē geese! Would you like to join my band?" The geese look at each other and say, "Honk, nay-nay, chirp, honk" and then go back to eating berries. They make a beautiful duet together, but they are not bandmates.

“Mahalo,” I sing out as I head back to the trail. “A hui hou!”

I arrive at Tūtū's house with no bandmate. I can't help the tears forming, but I look up and see Tūtū watching me from her front porch.

“Aloha, Alora!” she calls to me.

“Aloha, Tūtū,” I say as I wipe the tears now falling down my cheeks. “Can you come to the neighborhood lūʻau tonight?”

"I would love to come. But why so sad mo'opuna?" she asks as she hands me a plate of her famous mochi cake.

"Everyone wants me to play 'ukulele for the party, but I don't want to play by myself. I tried to find a bandmate, but no one seems right," I say before taking a big buttery bite.

Tūtū smiles big and says, "A little girl moved into the house next door and she doesn't know anyone in the neighborhood. She was outside earlier...playing her ʻukulele."

I can't believe it. "Tūtū, do you think she would be part of my band?" She winks at me and says, "Go over there and find out!"

“I will! Mahalo and see you tonight, Tūtū,” I call out as I head next door. I find the new neighbor sitting on her porch playing an ‘ukulele...and she is good!

"Aloha! I'm Alora. Would you like to join my band and play at the neighborhood lūʻau tonight?"

She looks at me and smiles. "Aloha, I'm Kaloka. I've never been in a band before, and I've never been to a neighborhood lūʻau. Do you think I'm good enough to be in your band?"

I sit down next to her and say, “So far I’ve asked the spinners dolphins, a monk seal, a green sea turtle, a hoary bat, and the nēnē geese, but none of them are right. You are perfect!”

Kaloka smiles and replies, “Let’s do it!” We both start playing our ‘ukulele together and coming up with songs to play at the lū‘au. I can tell we are going to be good friends.

"See you tonight! Aloha, Kaloka!" I say as I give her a hug. I skip and strum all the way home, waving as I pass the nēnē geese, hoary bat, green sea turtle, monk seal, and spinner dolphins.

The lūʻau is finally here! There is poi, macaroni salad, haupia, kālua pork cooked in an underground imu, and, of course, Tūtū's famous mochi cake. There is hula dancing, pineapple bowling, and singing. Kaloka and I are ready for our performance, and neither of us are nervous because we have each other. We even came up with a band name: The Ukulele Girls!

I have found the perfect bandmate...and the best part is, I have found a new friend.

End

GLOSSARY:

A hui hou (ah who-ee ho) - until we meet again

Aloha (ah-low-ha) - hello, goodbye, love, respect

Haupia (how-pee-uh) - Hawaiian coconut pudding

Imu (ee-moo) - Hawaiian underground oven

Kālua pork (kuh-loo-uh) - pork cooked in an underground oven

Lūʻau (loo-ow) - Hawaiian feast

Mahalo (ma-ha-low) - thank you

Malasada (mal-uh-sah-duh) - Portuguese fried yeast doughnuts coated with granulated sugar

Mochi (moh-chee) - soft, chewy Japanese rice cake

Moʻopuna (moh-oh-poo-nah) - grandchild

Nēnē (nay-nay) - Hawaiian goose

Poi (p-oy) - made from cooked taro and water; a purple pudding like side dish

Tūtū (too-too) - grandmother